ABSTRACT

This Book provides professionals with an historical perspective, data and possible solutions for organizations and employees alike to work life balance.

Work life balance has recently taken the attention of both researchers and executives. This subject interests almost everyone with a professional career. This widespread interest is partly due to its reflection on all aspects of life. For those who think that the main objective in life is to work, their career becomes the core of life and they fail to concentrate to their family or personal life.

However, people have limited time and therefore have to perform many other activities other than their jobs. Without a balance between the two, many mishaps can be experienced in both. In this study work –life balance is analyzed from organizational context. This study has the potential to enable the working people to consider their stand point in terms of work –life balance and the executives to gain new perspective in order to cope with such a problem.

By: Vijander Kumar (MBA HR Professional) India

And By: Brahmmanand Saraswati

July' 2018

E-mail: brahmmanandsaraswati@gmail.com

Work Life Balance

Before going through the knowledge of work life balance, I would like you to know and understand your dharma and meaning of Dharma. Best Dharma is described by lord Krishna to Arjuna at the time of Mahabharata. Following own dharma will lead you better, happy and successful life. Dharma gives better understanding and solutions regarding your work life and personal life. You will never have to re-think in your any life situation that what to do now? What is to be done in specific situation? If you have clear understanding of Dharma, the answers will automatically come out to you.

So it is better to keep understanding of Dharma in your mind all the time while you are going through understanding of work life balance.

What is Dharma?

There are *four* core concepts from the Gita which extolls the beautiful potential that exists vibrantly in each one of us and, indeed, in every atom of the entire cosmos, known and unknown, seen and unseen.

Concept one: Look to your Dharma

Dharma can mean "law of the universe," "social and religious rules," and/or one's own individual mission or purpose. On the individual level, it can also mean a number of things.

For example, in the Gita, Krishna points out to Arjuna that his Dharma is to be a warrior whether he likes it or not. He cannot escape his Dharma and he must fulfill it. Arjuna is a warrior for what is right and just. He is not just a warrior for fighting's sake. His Dharma must be grounded in a proper purpose.

"Whatever role we are fulfilling at the moment is our Dharma at that moment."

Concept two: Do it full out

Both Hinduism and Buddhism extoll this virtue of absolute commitment. In fact, many books have been written about the power of focus and single-mindedness, including the Gita. Success in life is no accident and it is a result of pursuing one's Dharma full out, no holding back.

Upon looking back, I see that I did not always carry out my Dharma as a husband and father and I have made mistakes that have impacted others' lives unfavorably. Had I had the vision to take the longer and broader view on things, I may not have made these mistakes. I feel that I was more concerned with material success at any cost, even if others had to pay a price. I now see that I was not acting properly in these and probably many other cases. In this current chapter of my life, I would like to pursue my new Dharma with more mindfulness and focus on proper context and big picture focus.

Concept three: Let go of the fruits of your labor

When we invest our efforts or resources, it tends to take on our self-identity in our minds. Subconsciously, we associate this identity with life/death. This mistaken association leads us to regard all critics or those who appear to get in our way as mortal threats to be neutralized, lest we "die."

The Gita exhorts us to release this incorrect view and to realize that our self and the phenomenal world at large are not real. What is real is "Self," the divine within all life, sentient and insentient. Even the air we breathe has the divine nestled in every particle. Therefore, instead of jealously guarding our self-worth, we are much better letting all that go and acting out of gratitude for the opportunity to work on our Dharma. Krishna says we our entitled to work, but not to any of the fruits of our work. When we adopt this attitude, all we can feel is gratitude, no matter what happens.

I have found that as I endeavor to embrace this concept, I am shown which areas need work and I am grateful to be shown these things and grateful to be able to improve so I can one day serve others with gratitude and without attachment to the fruits.

Concept four: Offer it all up to the divine

I feel this concept is closely related to its predecessor. How much easier it becomes to let go of the fruits when one is offering every moment up to the divine. The ultimate form of this is when one feels that God is acting through him/her. In truth, this is what is happening all the time, we just fail to see it and that failure results in suffering and angst.

"Reduce your wants and lead a happy and contented life. Never hurt the feelings of others and be kind to all. Think of God as soon as you get up and when you go to bed."

I believe this last sentence resonates with this fourth core concept from the Gita upon which this post is focused. It provides a very practical way to begin to incorporate this concept in one's life. Begin the day focused on God and end the day focused on God. What a beautiful way to live!

INTRODUCTION

Work-life balance is defined here as an individual's ability to meet their work and family commitments, as well as other responsibilities and activities. Work life balance, in addition to the relations between work and family functions, also involves other roles in other areas of life. In this study, due to its more extensive associations, the concept of work–life balance is preferred.

Life is a balancing act, and in American society, it is safe to say that almost everyone is seeking work/life balance. But what exactly is work/life balance? We have all heard the term, and many of us complain that we don't have enough of it in our lives. Among men and women alike, the frustrating search for work/life balance is a frequent topic of conversation, usually translated into not enough time and/or support to do, to handle, to manage ... our work commitments or personal responsibilities.

Work-life balance has been defined differently by different scholars. In order to broaden our perspectives, some definitions will be presented.

Greenhaus (2002) defined work –life balance as satisfaction and good functioning at work and at home with a minimum of role conflict.

Felstead et al. (2002) defines work-life balance as the relationship between the institutional and cultural times and spaces of work and non-work in societies where income is predominantly generated and distributed through labor markets.

Scholars defined life balance as fulfilling the demands satisfactorily in the three basic areas of life; namely, work, family and private.

Work demands work hours, work intensity and proportion of working hours spent in work.
Additional work hours subtract from home time, while high work intensity or work pressure may result in fatigue, anxiety or other adverse physiological consequences that affect the quality of home and family life.

In a society filled with conflicting responsibilities and commitments, work/life balance has become a predominant issue in the workplace. Three major factors contribute to the interest in, and the importance of, serious consideration of work/life balance:

1) Global competition; 2) renewed interest in personal lives/family values; and 3) an aging workforce. Research suggests that forward-thinking human resource professionals seeking innovative ways to augment their organization's competitive advantage in the marketplace may find that work/life balance challenges offer a win-win solution.

Work –life balance is not the allocation of time equally among work, family and personal demands. In literature, it is also emphasized that work-life balance is subjective phenomenon that changes from person to person.
In this regard, work-life balance should be regarded as allocating the available resources like time, thought and labor wisely among the elements of life. While some adopt the philosophy of 'working to live' and sees work as the objective, others consider "living to work" and situated work into the center of life.

DETERMINANTS OF WORK-LIFE BALANCE

Many things in life are the determinants of work life balance. The subjects in the literature that are related the most with work life balance are grouped here.

FAMILY

The demands that one experience in family life and that have effects on life balance can be given as the demand of workload and time, role expectations in family and support to be given to the spouse. It is also included in the literature that such variances as marriage, child rising, caring of the elderly at home have effect on work-life balance since they demand more family responsibilities. Those who have to look after a child or the elderly might sometimes have to risk their career by shortening their working hours, which becomes a source of stress for them. On the other hand, those without children or any elderly to look after at home experience less work-life imbalance.

WORK AND ORGANISATION

Work environment is more effective in work-life imbalance than the family environment. The job and the institution one works in both demands on his time, efforts and mental capacity. Among the efforts to increase organizational efficiency, one of the subjects managers focus on is to raise the organizational efficiency, one of the subjects managers focus on is to raise the organizational loyalty of the staff.

With the growing diversity of family structures represented in the workforce in the new millennium, it is important that professionals better understand the interface of work and family relationships and the resulting impact in the workplace.

Typically, studies have focused on employed men and women who are married or living with a partner or those with children. Omitted from research are single-earner mothers and fathers, single and childless employees with extensive responsibility for eldercare, blended families with children from both partners' prior marriages, families with shared custody of children, and grandparents raising their grandchildren.

Conflict between work and family has real consequences and significantly affects quality of family life and career attainment of both men and women. The consequences for women may include serious constraints on career choices, limited opportunity for career advancement and success in their work role, and the need to choose between two apparent opposites— an active and satisfying career or marriage and children. Many men have to trade off personal and career values while they search for ways to make dual career families work, often requiring them to embrace family roles that are far different, and more egalitarian, than those they learned as children. This research reveals a compensatory effect. Between two forms of psychological interference: work-to-family and family-to-work. Specifically, support from two domains (partner and employer) has a significant impact on one another. The impact of partner support is greater when business professionals feel their employers are unsupportive of their lives beyond work. Conversely, for employees with relatively unsupportive partners, the employer family-friendliness reduces role conflicts more than partners. Thus, one source of support compensates for the lack of the other.

SOCIAL ENVIRONMENT

Another determinant of work-life balance is social environment. Especially in countries that stand out with their culturally collectivist characteristics, an individual also has responsibilities towards certain social groups he belongs.

Being social is a fundamental part of human nature, without it we can become lost within an internal chaos that prevents us from moving forward and adapting to changes that happen around us. If socializing is a vital part of everyday life, why wouldn't this ring true for the work environment too?

From my experience, establishing a social structure within the workplace is an imperative component in achieving a productive, hardworking and happy organization. It extends far beyond going for a drink or bite to eat after work with colleagues, to include how colleagues and even management interact with each other on a daily basis.

Establishing a social working environment enables you, as an employer, to create a cohesive and unified community, which is built upon a mutual sense of respect, trust and support. Within a business context, a social community provides a chance for colleagues to share their issues and concerns with their fellow co-workers, whilst also celebrating positive aspects within the organization. It is important that this social community steers away from focusing on any negativity in the work environment regarding colleague working relationships, as this can have an adverse effect on team morale and actually discourage employee cooperation, resulting in dissension among the workforce.

Incorporating a social element into your organizational structure also serves as an effective method to help reduce stress and tension within the workplace. If the saying 'a problem shared is a problem halved' is true, then facilitating the open expression of queries and issues regarding current work projects can only be a positive step forward. Work stress can often build through work overload, particularly from impending deadlines. If employees are encouraged to communicate with their colleagues and management through scheduled meetings or spur of the moment discussions, then the chances of stress levels escalating beyond control greatly diminishes, thus helping the workplace become more productive and efficient.

From a business perspective, ***if employees enjoy coming to work and have a high degree of job satisfaction, the effects of this will go beyond the internal dynamics of an organization and filter out to how customers or clients perceive your business.*** With a social environment helping to facilitate a happy workforce, clients and customers are more likely to view your company as a positive, cooperative and professional organization, consequently encouraging them to provide continued loyalty and speak favorably about your company gaining positive word of mouth. Conversely, if an organization fosters a culture whereby employees feel isolated, overworked and unhappy in their job, then this will likely lead to the development of a negative reputation stemming from employee attitudes and behavior.

CONSEQUENCES OF WORK-LIFE IMBALANCE

The stress – based conflict occurs when one of the roles of the individual at work or in the family causes stress on the individual and this stress affects the other roles of the individual. The behavior stress occurs when the behavior at work and out of work are dissonant and conflicting.

It may be tempting to rack up those extra hours at work, however if you're spending most of your time working, though, your home life will definitely take a hit.

Poor work-life balance can lead to some serious consequences such as:

- **Fatigue**: If you are over tired it reduces your ability to work productively and think clearly. This can take a toll on your professional reputation.
- **Health**: Long working hours can cause stress which may have adverse effects on one's immune system. Stress also puts one at risk of substance abuse.
- **No time for Family:** Working long hours or overtime might make you miss important family moments and events. This can leave you feeling left out and damage your relationships.
- **Increased Expectations:** Working extra hours might lead to you taking on extra responsibility. This can cause extra stress and challenges that one will have a really hard time facing.

When asked about why we work overtime and such long hours, most of us answer that it is out of our control.

Even if you don't have much control over the hours you have to work, you can **ask yourself: In what other ways am I bringing greater enjoyment into my life?**

One needs to focus your time and attention on things you can control.

Work life balancing Techniques

Here are 5 tips you can use to bring a little more balance into your daily routine:

Add downtime into your busy schedule

When you plan your week, make it a point to schedule time with your loved ones and friends as well as activities that will help you recharge and give you more energy like going to the gym. Time spent with your family and friends should also be adventurous and fun such as date night with your spouse or paintball with your friends. You'll have something to look forward to and manage your time better so you don't have to cancel.

Drop activities that drain your energy

Many people waste their time and energy on people that add no value. Such as spending too much time at work with that one colleague who constantly just wants to vent and gossip.

You need to become aware of activities that don't enhance your career and personal life and minimize the time you spend on these activities.

Rethink your tasks

Consider whether you can outsource any of your time-consuming household chores like ordering your groceries online instead of going to the shop to buy them and asking the boy down the street to mow your lawn for a small fee. Even if you're on a tight budget, you may discover that the time you'll save will make it worth it. But it's this saved time that you need to use resourcefully like spending it with your family, creating memories and building relationships.

Get moving

It's hard to make time for exercise when you have a jam-packed schedule, but it may ultimately help you get more done by boosting your energy level and ability to concentrate. Whatever you are doing try to enjoy the moment and whatever is gone from your hand just leave it and keep moving and try to make best what comes ahead.

A little relaxation goes a very long way

Don't assume that you need to make big changes to bring more balance to your life. Set small realistic goals to get to the overall big goal you want to achieve. Start small like decide to leave the office one night early per week. Slowly build more activities into your week that are important to you and your health. Even during a hectic day, you can take just 10 or 15 minutes to do something that will recharge your batteries like reading a book or going for a walk.

Most importantly, know when to seek professional help. Everyone needs help from time to time. If your life feels too chaotic to manage and you're spinning your wheels worrying about it, talk with a professional — such as a Counselor or Life Coach. We at Capacity Trust offer these services and want to help you grow your capacity to find a better work-life balance.

If your employer offers employee assistance programs, take advantage of the available services. Or if you feel your employer needs to implement new employee wellness programs then let them give us a call so we can help and work on not just improving your daily life but everyone in your company's as well.

The results of the study indicate that although the effects of a poor work-life balance may not be felt immediately, the consequences extend into older age.

Cutting down on work hours and getting plenty of rest as early in life as possible would mitigate adverse health effects in older age.

ORGANIZATIONAL PERSPECTIVE

In order to decrease the negative consequences of work-family conflict on working individuals, family friendly organizational culture and human resources applications have recently been in agenda of executive. The components of the organizational strategy are flexible working hours, child care and elderly care scheme, home working ,job sharing. Supportive programs for the family life of employees in an organization contribute to providing work –life balance. Thanks to these programs, the employees will be encouraged, their attendance will be supported and their efficiency will increase. Flexible working hours is one of the methods used to maintain work-life balance.

Conclusion

If one has managed to allocate the required time for every aspect of life duly and not to reflect the problems in one part of life to another it means that he has been able to achieve work- Family balance. Life as a whole is composed of many other aspects along with work. Those who have achieved a balance among these aspects are sure to achieve the life balance, which does away with any imbalance.

In Other point of view

Is Your Organization Culture-Ready for Work/Life Initiatives?

"A common thread that links the reasons work/life benefits go unused is organizational culture."

Before establishing work/life initiatives, it is important to know if the organization's culture is open and ready to support work/life programs. The path to determining culture readiness may be as formal as using an employee survey assessment or as simple as a thoughtful judgment made by the organization. The following provides food for thought regarding whether an organization is ready to begin work/life initiatives.

As with most change initiatives, work/life programs require support from senior management. In addition, for the work environment to be ready for work/life benefits, it is helpful to have a *"corporate culture that encourages employees to look at business in an entirely different way and supports and accepts employees as individuals with priorities beyond the workplace."*

"Life cycles are another consideration. People need different things at different times of their lives,"

Employers are realizing that work should be intrinsically interesting and satisfying to employees, and these are the folks who produce the best work. The manager's job is to get out of the way. The move from extrinsic rewards to intrinsic rewards has an impact on work/life initiatives.

One of the challenges of work/life initiatives—from both the employer and the employee viewpoint—is equitability, which has been cited as a major concern regarding work/life initiatives. When organizations are establishing work/life programs, it is important to consider the purpose of the programs and whom they serve. For example, do the work/life programs serve all employees or are they aimed toward employees who are parents or who are dealing with their elderly parents?

To determine the culture readiness of an organization for work/life initiatives, the researchers developed a series of questions to measure supportive work/life culture, addressing perceived managerial support, negative career consequences for devoting time to family concerns, and organizational time demands and expectations that interfere with family responsibilities. The study revealed that more work/family benefits translated to greater commitment, less work/family conflict, and less intention to leave. Interestingly, the study results confirmed anecdotal evidence that a supportive work/family culture is closely related to work attitudes and perceived managerial support linked with less intention to leave the organization.

Work/Life Balance in the Relief World

In the "relief world," comprised of organizations with employees and volunteers that provide service and care to communities in need locally and worldwide, the demands of an aging population in the coming decade are increasing the current strong competition for qualified individuals upon which relief organizations depend. "Not only will there be fewer young, keen and free-to-travel individuals who will want to be convinced that agencies are caring, 'best-practice' employers, but more skills and experience will be possessed by older staff likely to have families and other commitments and thus different priorities for their work/life balance." Therefore, organizations that provide relief services may experience increasing difficulty staffing and retaining employees due to the pull of family commitments at home.

Furthermore, the challenges of work/life balance will no doubt impact recruitment, retention and willingness to serve in hardship locations. In view of these factors, voluntary organizations and aid agencies whose missions and services are critical in many parts of the world may well have an even greater need for work/life programs to attract and retain staff.

Total Life Planning

Total life planning is a new and innovative approach to work/life benefits and helps employees examine important aspects of their professional and personal lives and understand how they relate. Their goal is "to encourage employees to look at their lives as a whole and assess relationships, emotional and physical wellbeing, careers, spirituality, and their personal financial situation. From these programs, employees can assess their available choices to improve balance in their lives and develop an individualized life plan … the most successful programs set a goal-oriented environment with a meaningful and transformational component for each individual."

The concept of total life planning represents a paradigm shift in our society. One of the major benefits is renewed employee energy, enthusiasm for work, and increased productivity. Total life planning programs may be offered in conjunction with benefits such as health, life, and disability insurance, or on a standalone basis. However, not all organizations may wish to consider total life planning, as it brings topics into the workplace that have traditionally been considered private.

Conclusion

Work/life programs have the potential to significantly improve employee morale, reduce absenteeism, and retain organizational knowledge, particularly during difficult economic times. In today's global marketplace, as companies aim to reduce costs, it falls to the human resource professional to understand the critical issues of work/life balance and champion work/life programs. Be it employees whose family members and/or friends are called to serve their country, single mothers who are trying to raise their children and make a living, Generation X and Y employees who value their personal time, couples struggling to manage dual-career marriages, or companies losing critical knowledge when employees leave for other opportunities, work/life programs offer a win-win situation for employers and employees.

Some tips for better work-life balance

According to Maslow's hierarchy, your needs should be satisfied sequentially. First come the survival needs of food, water and shelter, followed by emotional needs of safety, love, belonging to a group and self-esteem. Going to work earns you money for basic needs and surrounds you with people, thus partially providing for emotional needs.

The next category constitutes mental and creative needs for knowledge, beauty and achieving one's full potential. Only a well-planned lifestyle with adequate personal time can fulfil these. Working round the clock causes stress, poor health and burnout. Instead, try to achieve a better work-life balance. Here's how.

- Choose three

    Randi Zuckerberg – the sibling of Facebook's founder – says that one can pick only three things out of work, sleep, family, friends and fitness. It is important to know what really matters to you and to prioritize it. Define the parameters of success in each area you choose and consciously distribute time among multiple goals. Learn to say 'no' to people and activities that distract you from your priorities.

- Draw your clock

    Use a diary to track how you spend the hours of your workday as well as on a holiday. Put those hours in different buckets – work, family, and chores, fun – and categorize each task into urgent/not urgent and important/not important. Draw a circle with different segments representing each bucket. This is your current life. Now draw new circles to represent your ideal workday and holiday and mark out your desired segments. Work on moving from your current to your ideal clock. Focus on eliminating unimportant tasks and completing important tasks on time.

- Small steps

    Do not make more than two small changes a week and give yourself time to settle into new routines. Sudden major changes die out quickly. Start with baby steps. Keep at it consistently for three weeks and you have formed a new habit.

- Mind and body

    If you are constantly stressed, your work life balance needs fixing. The best way to de-stress is to focus on your body and mind. Daily physical exercise triggers the release of endorphins, which relieve stress. Similarly, meditation, music, a hobby or enjoyable companionship can enable your mind to disengage from stressful thoughts, at least temporarily.

- Look for change

    Do not assume that your lifestyle has no scope for improvement. Ask yourself what changes to your routine would improve your balance. Can you schedule client meetings in off-peak hours, so you spend less time in traffic? Can you order groceries online instead of spending an hour in the market? Create habits that ensure good nutrition, sleep and exercise. Build support systems within your family and team that help you out when you need it and enable better time utilization.

- <u>Unplug</u>

    Designate a certain amount of time to 'unplug' yourself from your mobile phone and the Internet. These two either keep you hooked to work or to useless activities that prevent you from important activities like getting enough rest, spending quality time with people you connect with, and engaging in things that make you happy and help you relax.

- <u>Don't multi-task</u>

    Say 'no' to multi-tasking. This can dramatically reduce stress and improve outcomes at work and in your personal life. Draw a rigid boundary around anything that you are currently doing. If you are having dinner with your family switch off all distractions and be there for them. If you are in a team meeting do not look at your cell phone to read e-mails. If your mind is constantly wandering, maybe you should not be on the current task.

- <u>One hour a day</u>

    Finally, respect yourself. Set aside an hour every day for yourself and respect that time as much as you would respect your manager's time. Use that hour to build a habit of your choice. This is your daily down time which is sacrosanct, except during emergencies. This time will help you recharge and restore balance.

Causes of imbalance

1. **Societal expectations**

   Society sets unrealistic targets for us, which causes unnecessary stress. As a result, you might experience distress on getting average marks in an exam, not earning enough or failing to fulfill family obligations. To avoid this, learn to distinguish between social conditioning and your priorities.

2. **Extreme ambition**

   Single-minded ambition regarding work comes from internal triggers or from a need for social recognition and success. However, it inevitably leads to hiding failures, avoiding people and ultimately becoming cynical and unhappy. Substitute it with moderated ambition aimed at achieving multiple parallel work and life goals.

3. **Desperate for perfection**

   Social media platforms like Instagram and Facebook show us a false image of the glamorous lives that other people lead. Their lives seem full of impeccable fashion, family, friends, food and fun. If you are seeking total perfection in any area of life, know that it takes time away from other things, leading to greater imbalance and unhappiness.

4. <u>Denied depression</u>

Depression and burnout are socially unacceptable weaknesses. As a result of this taboo, these issues are ignored and rarely shared with others. This leads to rapid deterioration without any attempt to address the causes. Recognize them as mental ailments in both yourself and loved ones, and seek therapy or make lifestyle changes as needed.

5. <u>One size fits all</u>

In a crowded and competitive world, uniform rules are applied to everyone for the sake of 'fairness'. In schools everyone studies all subjects at the same pace. Fixed policies at work leave little room for you to control your life. Try to choose a career and employers that fit your life, not someone else's.

-: Adopt These 12 Habits for a Better Work-Life Balance:-

1. Understand what "balance" means.

Stand straight up with your feet a little ways apart. Now, lean over significantly to the right. Are you still standing? I hope so! You haven't lost your balance -- even though your right foot is taking significantly more weight. This just goes to show that "balance" doesn't mean "equal." Sometimes, either work or your personal life takes more weight, depending on what's going on at the moment -- and that's OK.

2. Let go of fear.

To develop a healthy balance between work and life, you have to first let go of the fear that, if you're not working, your company will fail. When you've done a day's work, let it go, rest and try again tomorrow. The sky will not fall on you -- even if you've left several items unchecked on your to-do list.

3. Schedule important personal activities.

Things such as exercise, date nights with a spouse and more can quickly fall by the wayside if they aren't purposefully scheduled. Block out your calendar for important personal events, and you'll find they happen as they should. It can be tough to remember in the middle of a stressful business moment, but they're just as important as any meeting.

4. Set boundaries.

If customers or colleagues think it's OK to call you at 11 p.m. if they need something, they will. Set firm boundaries around when you are, and aren't, available. Doing so will help you relax when you're off the clock and avoid burnout, while also helping others avoid unmet expectations.

If you've previously kept an open door policy at all hours of the day, shifting to a more limited availability can be frustrating to people who are used to having continuous access to you. Notify them of your schedule changes in a professional manner and reiterate that limiting your availability will improve your ability to meet their needs more effectively when you are "on the clock."

5. Think carefully about where you live.

Warren Buffett told MBA students a few years ago that the reason he chose to live in Omaha -- rather than New York or other cities closer to the financial scene -- was because Omaha helped him maintain a more balanced life. Even if you can't choose your city, you can choose your neighborhood. Do so with your ideal work-life balance in mind.

6. Turn off technology.

With smartphones and increasing demands on workers, we now live in an "always on" culture. However, you have power over your devices. Be intentional about turning them off (not just on silent) and taking technology breaks. It will help you tremendously by keeping you more focused during your productive periods.

7. Manage your energy, not your time.

Every human being has natural energy cycles throughout the day. If you think carefully about your own cycles, you'll probably be able to pinpoint times when you usually feel more focused and productive, as well as times where you'd rather crawl into bed than spend another minute at the computer.

Instead of trying to schedule every minute of your time and push through your low-energy cycles, schedule your tasks according to your energy. Do lower-energy administrative tasks when you're in a lull, and more important work when you're energized.

8. Schedule vacation time.

I know that you're busy and that your business is demanding, but if big corporations can make vacation time happen, then so can you. Remember, vacation time doesn't have to involve a week-long tropical getaway (although if you can afford the expense and the time away from the office, that's a great way to recharge). Even a day away from the office can be enough to leave you feeling re-focused and refreshed.

If you're so involved in your business you feel you really can't be gone, even for a day, it's time to learn to delegate. Contrary to what you might believe, you aren't the only one who can handle many of the tasks you currently spend time on. Your team members will feel empowered if you shuffle additional responsibilities to them, and you'll finally get to relax.

9. Join social groups.

If you find it hard to socialize because you're always working, consider joining a social-only group. You can check out Meetup.com for groups in your area, or join a non-business related sports team or bowling league. Focus on using these opportunities to meet new friends, not on talking shop.

10. Delegate household tasks.

If you have the ability and extra cash to do so, consider hiring out or delegating household tasks. For example, a housekeeper who comes once a week can help you tackle the cleaning projects that always seem to pile up, while a lawn service can save you the hours that you'd otherwise spend mowing your grass or maintaining you're landscaping.

By looking for and taking advantage of opportunities such as these, you'll be able to spend your personal time with friends and family, instead of doing chores. Or, if your spouse or older children can handle some of the more mundane tasks while you work, you can all enjoy having fun together afterward.

11. Use calendar blocks for laser focus.

You have a calendar, so use it. Schedule specific blocks of uninterrupted time for your most important tasks. If you work in an office, make sure your fellow workers know to leave you alone during this time. Shut the door to your office, turn down your phone's ringer and turn off the email and text notifications that are constantly interrupting your work. Use your scheduled blocks for work that's laser focused on the tasks and projects that matter most for your business.

12. Limit your work hours.

Work never ends, and if you're looking to finish everything, you'll never stop. Working long hours isn't good for anyone -- you, your family or your colleagues. Sheryl Sandberg spent years leaving work at 5:30 to have dinner with her children. If she can do it, why can't you?

Work-life balance is not a system of having your work and life take exactly the same amount of hours or focus. It's a way of making sure that both your work priorities and your personal priorities are being met. Sometimes that means more work hours, and other times it means less. In either situation, in developing the 12 habits listed above, you'll be well on your way to developing and maintaining a great work-life balance.

Other way to understand work and life:

At Work

- **Set manageable goals each day.** Being able to meet priorities helps us feel a sense of accomplishment and control. The latest research shows that the more control we have over our work, the less stressed we get. So be realistic about workloads and deadlines. Make a "to do" list, and take care of important tasks first and eliminate unessential ones. Ask for help when necessary.

- **Be efficient with your time at work.** When we procrastinate, the task often grows in our minds until it seems insurmountable. So when you face a big project at work or home, start by dividing it into smaller tasks. Complete the first one before moving on to the next. Give yourself small rewards upon each completion, whether it's a five minute break or a walk to the coffee shop. If you feel overwhelmed by routines that seem unnecessary, tell your boss. The less time you spend doing busy work or procrastinating, the more time you can spend productively, or with friends or family.

- **Ask for flexibility.** Flex time and telecommuting are quickly becoming established as necessities in today's business world, and many companies are drafting work/life policies. If you ask, they might allow you to work flexible hours or from home a day a week. Research shows that employees who work flexible schedules are more productive and loyal to their employers.

- **Take five.** Taking a break at work isn't only acceptable, it's often encouraged by many employers. Small breaks at work—or on any project—will help clear your head, and improve your ability to deal with stress and make good decisions when you jump back into the grind.

- **Tune in.** Listen to your favorite music at work to foster concentration, reduce stress and anxiety, and stimulate creativity. Studies dating back more than 30 years show the benefits of music in everyday life, including lowered blood pressure. Be sure to wear headphones on the job, and then pump up the volume—and your productivity.

- **Communicate effectively.** Be honest with colleagues or your boss when you feel you're in a bind. Chances are, you're not alone. But don't just complain—suggest practical alternatives. Looking at a situation from someone else's viewpoint can also reduce your stress. In a tense situation, either rethink your strategy or stand your ground, calmly and rationally. Make allowances for other opinions, and compromise. Retreat before you lose control, and allow time for all involved to cool off. You'll be better equipped to handle the problem constructively later.

- **Give yourself a break.** No one's perfect! Allow yourself to be human and just do the best you can.

At Home

- **Unplug.** The same technology that makes it so easy for workers to do their jobs flexibly can also burn us out if we use them 24/7. By all means, make yourself available—especially if you've earned the right to "flex" your hours—but recognize the need for personal time, too.

- **Divide and conquer.** Make sure responsibilities at home are evenly distributed and clearly outlined— you'll avoid confusion and problems later.

- **Don't over commit.** Do you feel stressed when you just glance at your calendar? If you're overscheduled with activities, learn to say," No." Shed the superman/superwoman urge!

- **Get support.** Chatting with friends and family can be important to your success at home—or at work—and can even improve your health. People with stronger support systems have more aggressive immune responses to illnesses than those who lack such support.

- **Take advantage of your company's Employee Assistance Program (EAP).** Many organizations offer resources through an EAP, which can save you precious time by providing guidance on issues like where to find a daycare center and caretaking for an elderly parent, as well as referrals to mental health and other services.

- **Stay active.** Aside from its well-known physical benefits, regular exercise reduces stress, depression and anxiety, and enables people to better cope with adversity, according to researchers. It'll also boost your immune system and keep you out of the doctor's office. Make time in your schedule for the gym or to take a walk during lunch—and have some fun!

- **Treat your body right.** Being in good shape physically increases your tolerance to stress and reduces sick days. Eat right, exercise and get adequate rest. Don't rely on drugs, alcohol or cigarettes to cope with stress; they'll only lead to more problems.

- **Get help if you need it.** Don't let stress stand in the way of your health and happiness. If you are persistently overwhelmed, it may be time to seek help from a mental health professional. Asking for help is not a sign of weakness—taking care of yourself is a sign of strength.

Know when to seek professional help

Everyone needs help from time to time. If your life feels too chaotic to manage and you're spinning your wheels worrying about it, talk with a professional — such as a counselor or other mental health provider. If your employer offers an employee assistance program, take advantage of available services.

Remember, striking a healthy work-life balance isn't a one-shot deal. Creating work-life balance is a continuous process as your family, interests and work life change. Periodically examine your priorities — and make changes, if necessary — to make sure you're keeping on track.

Staying positive also make you stronger and achiever

3 Powerful Ways to Stay Positive

We've all received the well-meaning advice to "stay positive." The greater the challenge, the more this glass-half-full wisdom can come across as Pollyannaish and unrealistic. It's hard to find the motivation to focus on the positive when positivity seems like nothing more than wishful thinking.

The real obstacle to positivity is that our brains are hard-wired to look for and focus on threats. This survival mechanism served humankind well back when we were hunters and gatherers, living each day with the very real threat of being killed by someone or something in our immediate surroundings.

That was eons ago. Today, this mechanism breeds pessimism and negativity through the mind's tendency to wander until it finds a threat. These "threats" magnify the perceived likelihood that things are going—and/or are going to go—poorly. When the threat is real and lurking in the bushes down the path, this mechanism serves you well. When the threat is imagined and you spend two months convinced the project you're working on is going to flop, this mechanism leaves you with a soured view of reality that wreaks havoc in your life.

Maintaining positivity is a daily challenge that requires focus and attention. You must be intentional about staying positive if you're going to overcome the brain's tendency to focus on threats. It won't happen by accident. That's why positivity is the skill that I'll be giving extra attention in 2018.

Positivity and Your Health

Pessimism is trouble because it's bad for your health. Numerous studies have shown that optimists are physically and psychologically healthier than pessimists.

Martin Seligman at the University of Pennsylvania has conducted extensive research on the topic. Seligman worked with researchers from Dartmouth and the University of Michigan on a study that followed people from age 25 to 65 to see how their levels of pessimism or optimism influenced their overall health. The researchers found that pessimists' health deteriorated far more rapidly as they aged.

Seligman's findings are similar to research conducted by the Mayo Clinic that found optimists have lower levels of cardiovascular disease and longer life-spans. Although the exact mechanism through which pessimism affects health hasn't been identified, researchers at Yale and the University of Colorado found that pessimism is associated with a weakened immune response to tumors and infection.

Researchers from the University of Kentucky went so far as to inject optimists and pessimists with a virus to measure their immune response. The researchers found optimists had a much stronger immune response than pessimists.

Positivity and Performance

Keeping a positive attitude isn't just good for your health. Martin Seligman has also studied the connection between positivity and performance. In one study in particular, he measured the degree to which insurance salespeople were optimistic or pessimistic in their work. Optimistic salespeople sold 37% more policies than pessimists, who were twice as likely to leave the company during their first year of employment.

Seligman has studied positivity more than anyone, and he believes in the ability to turn pessimistic thoughts and tendencies around with simple effort and know-how. But Seligman doesn't just believe this. His research shows that people can transform a tendency toward pessimistic thinking into positive thinking through simple techniques that create lasting changes in behavior long after they are discovered.

Here are three things that I'll be doing this year to stay positive.

1. Separate Fact from Fiction

The first step in learning to focus on the positive requires knowing how to stop negative self-talk in its tracks. The more you ruminate on negative thoughts, the more power you give them. Most of our negative thoughts are just that — thoughts, not facts.

When you find yourself believing the negative and pessimistic things your inner voice says, it's time to stop and write them down. Literally stop what you're doing and write down what you're thinking. Once you've taken a moment to slow down the negative momentum of your thoughts, you will be more rational and clear-headed in evaluating their veracity. Evaluate these statements to see if they're factual. You can bet the statements aren't true any time you see words like never, always, worst, ever, etc.

Do you really always lose your keys? Of course not. Perhaps you forget them frequently, but most days you do remember them. Are you never going to find a solution to your problem? If you really are that stuck, maybe you've been resisting asking for help. Or if it really is an intractable problem, then why are you wasting your time beating your head against the wall? If your statements still look like facts once they're on paper, take them to a friend or colleague you can trust, and see if he or she agrees with you. Then the truth will surely come out.

When it feels like something always or never happens, this is just your brain's natural threat tendency inflating the perceived frequency or severity of an event. Identifying and labeling your thoughts as thoughts by separating them from the facts will help you escape the cycle of negativity and move toward a positive new outlook.

2. Identify a Positive

Once you snap yourself out of self-defeating, negative thoughts, it's time to help your brain learn what you want it to focus on — the positive.

This will come naturally after some practice, but first you have to give your wandering brain a little help by consciously selecting something positive to think about. Any positive thought will do to refocus your brain's attention. When things are going well, and your mood is good, this is relatively easy. When things are going poorly, and your mind is flooded with negative thoughts, this can be a challenge. In these moments, think about your day and identify one positive thing that happened, no matter how small. If you can't think of something from the current day, reflect on the previous day or even the previous week. Or perhaps there is an exciting event you are looking forward to that you can focus your attention on.

The point here is you must have something positive that you're ready to shift your attention to when your thoughts turn negative. Step one stripped the power from negative thoughts by separating fact from fiction. Step two is to replace the negative with a positive. Once you have identified a positive thought, draw your attention to that thought each time you find yourself dwelling on the negative. If that proves difficult, you can repeat the process of writing down the negative thoughts to discredit their validity, and then allow yourself to freely enjoy positive thoughts.

3. Cultivate an Attitude of Gratitude

Taking time to contemplate what you're grateful for isn't merely the "right" thing to do; it reduces the stress hormone cortisol by 23%. Research conducted at the University of California, Davis, found that people who worked daily to cultivate an attitude of gratitude experienced improved mood, energy and substantially less anxiety due to lower cortisol levels.

You cultivate an attitude of gratitude by taking time out every day to focus on the positive. Any time you experience negative or pessimistic thoughts, use this as a cue to shift gears and think about something positive. In time, a positive attitude will become a way of life.

Bringing It All Together

Ask yourself the right questions.

This is the simplest but perhaps also the most important habit I have discovered in adopting an optimistic mindset. The questions we ask ourselves day in and day out when we wind up in negative, difficult or uncertain situations make all the difference in our life.

A pessimist might ask him/herself questions like:

- "Why did this happen to me?"
- "Why do bad things happen to me all the time?"

But an optimist asks him/herself the questions that open up the mind to new viewpoints and possibilities. A few of my favorite questions for finding the optimistic perspective are:

- "What is one good thing about this situation?"
- "What can I learn from this situation?"

- "What is one small step I can take today to start solving this situation?"

Create a positive environment to live in.

The people you spend your time with and the information you let influence your mind will have a huge effect on your attitude and how you think about things.

So choose to:

Spend more time with the people who lift you up. And less time – or no time – with people who just bring you down by being negative and critical. Read: You are the Average of the 5 People You Spend the Most Time With

Let in the information that supports you. Spend less time on negative and self-esteem damaging media sources and spend more time reading positive and constructive blogs and books, watching motivating movies, listening to inspirational songs, and listening to audio books and podcasts created by optimistic people. Check out 12 Inspirational Movies with Important Life Lessons to Learn and 25 Most Inspirational Songs of All Time.

Be grateful for what you have (don't forget about yourself too).

A very simple and quick way to boost the positive energy in your life is to tap into gratitude.

I usually do it by asking one or more of these questions:

1. What can I be grateful for in my life today?
2. Who are 3 people that I can be grateful to have in my life and why?
3. What are 3 things I can be grateful for about myself?

Just spend 60 seconds or a few minutes during your day with answering one of these questions to reap the wonderful benefits.

Don't forget about your physical self.

Being an optimist isn't just about thinking in a different way. It is also about caring for the physical part of ourselves.

I have found that working out a couple of times a week, enough quality sleep each night and eating healthy food has a huge effect on my mindset.

If I mismanage those very basic things then negative thoughts pop up far more often and I become more pessimistic and shut down about the possibilities in my life.

So don't neglect these basic fundamentals. Just caring for your physical self the right way can minimize a whole bunch of problems in life.

Start your day in an optimistic way.

The way you start your morning can set the tone for the rest of your day. For example, a stress-free morning often leads to less stress during the rest of the day.

So how can you set an optimistic tone for your day?

A three-step combination that has worked very well for me is to ask myself a gratitude question during breakfast, read some positive information online or in a book very early in the morning and then follow that up with exercising.

This sets my mind on the right path and fills me up with energy for my day.

Reduce your worries.

The worrying habit is a powerful and destructive one and can take over anyone's thinking. It used to be one of my biggest obstacles to optimism and to moving forward in life.

Two effective steps that have helped me and still help me to this day to minimize the worries are:

1. **Ask yourself: how many of my worries ever happened in reality?** If you are like me you will find that the answer is: very few. Most of the things you fear throughout your life will never happen. They are just nightmares or monsters in your own mind. This question can help you to do a reality check, to calm down and to realize that you

have most likely just been building another imaginary nightmare.
2. **Focus on solutions and the action you can take.** The worries grow stronger in a foggy mind and an inactive body. So use the questions in Steps 1 and 6 to move out of your worries and into resolution.

Don't let ideals ruin things.

A common mistake people make when making a shift in their attitudes is that they think that they have be perfect and do things perfectly all the time. This traps them from being positive.

Changing to a positive attitude can be gradual. While you may slip and stumble, continuing this way over time will strengthen your positive viewpoint more and more.

But if you set an inhuman standard for yourself and think you have to go from being a pessimist to always being an optimist, then you may find it hard to live up to that. And so you may feel like a failure. You get angry with yourself. And you may even give up on changing this habit and fall back into negative thinking.

So instead, focus on gradual change. If you are optimistic 40% of the time right now, try to improve this to being optimistic 60% of the time. Then, increase that to 80% when you are used to the new standard, then subsequently 100% if you can.

This focus on gradual improvement is far more sustainable and likely to bring long-term success than trying to reach an inhuman standard grounded in perfection.

Finally, a reminder to help you to not give up.

I would like to end this article with a simple but powerful and timeless thought that comforted and encouraged me to continue on when things looked bleak.

That thought is: *It is always darkest before the dawn.*

This thought has helped me to hold on and keep going when my social skills and dating life was just plain bad. It has helped me to continue on in my online business when things looked like they would never pick up. It has helped me to put one foot over another even when things looked dark.

I have found this thought to be very true. Why? Because when things seemed to be at the lowest for my blog, business, dating life or life in general, something positive would always happened. That's probably because being at a low point forced me to change how I did things.

But maybe also because life has a way of evening itself out when I go on. By taking action rather than give up, something good will always happens.

Seeing this thought live itself out has strengthened my belief in staying optimistic, in taking action and to keep going even when going through rough patches.

Ways to Stay Positive at Work

1. Keep learning.

Just because you're not in school anymore and you have a job, you don't have to stop learning. On-the-job education is the best way to build up your resume. Learn as much as you can from every work experience you have, from presenting during a meeting to giving a tour of your workplace to outsiders. If you don't have a chance to learn from new things, ask your coworkers or bosses if you can accompany them when they do their duties, and learn about what they do.

2. Teach others what you know.

You want to accompany others when they do their jobs, so offer that opportunity to your coworkers. Instead of helping them out only when they ask, offer to teach them what you know so they won't have to call you all of the time. It might feel good to be needed (talk about job security!), but when you have your own list of tasks to do, being called to help someone else can be inconvenient. You know what they say: "Give a man a fish and you feed him for a day; teach him how to fish and you have fed him for a lifetime."

3. Give yourself a break.

You're on the clock for eight hours a day, and you're expected to work that entire time, but you can't really do that. Trying to work nonstop means you're wearing yourself out, and each subsequent task you do will get a little sloppier as you lose focus and motivation. Take a short break every hour or two. Step away from your desk and stretch, get some fresh air. You might spend five to fifteen minutes not working, but you'll feel so refreshed by the time you come back to your office that you'll be ready to get to work immediately.

4. Leave work at work.

It's important to have time to yourself, your family, and your hobbies. If you work for eight hours, clock out, and then come home to do more work, you're not going to be excited to go back to work the next day. Make a rule where you have to leave your work at the office. If you don't complete a task while you're clocked in, make it a priority for the next morning, but leave it at work. It's hard not to even think about work while you're at home because it's such a large portion of your life, but give it a try. The more you put it out of your mind, the more rejuvenated you'll feel each morning when it's time to go back to the office.

5. Build relationships with coworkers.

Your work environment will be more comfortable and fun if you're friendly with your coworkers. You don't have to know every detail of their personal lives, or even the names of their children, but having a good back and forth with coworkers, bosses, and associates will make your workplace more inviting. Having a friendly community at work will also make you feel more supported in your work duties, which can help cut stress levels.

6. Participate in after-work activities.

When the clock strikes five, you're more than ready to go home, but don't let this attitude take over and leave you out of work events. If some of the crew are going out for dinner or drinks, tag along every once in a while. This helps build a community in the workplace, and you'll feel more connected to your coworkers. After all, you might still be with work people, but you won't be at work, so you'll still feel like you're having time outside of the office for yourself.

7. Make your workplace nice.

Whether you have an office, a cubicle, a classroom, or a desk in the middle of a crowded room, make your workplace nice! Check with your boss to see what kind of decorations are allowed, and then bring in some posters that motivate you, or family pictures that make you smile. Even something as small as bringing in your own coffee mug instead of using a Styrofoam cup can make your desk seem more homey. Sitting in an environment that looks nice and makes you feel good will do wonders for your motivation.

8. Volunteer to spearhead a project.

Instead of waiting to be assigned a project and getting stuck with something you might not like, why not volunteer to take on a project? This way you'll have more control over your tasks and you'll look great to your bosses. They'll be thrilled that you've willingly taken on more work, and will be more likely to consider you for the best of future projects and maybe even promotions.

9. Concentrate on one thing at a time.

You have a lot of things on your To Do list, but concentrating on one thing at a time will help you be more motivated and focused. If you stay on task until it's finished, you won't lose time by multitasking or changing course from one topic to another. By concentrating on one thing at a time, you also are more likely to complete more tasks fully, instead of doing bits and pieces of a bunch of different projects but not finishing any.

10. Set attainable goals.

Instead of setting your sights on the moon, set attainable work goals. It's good to have dreams, but if you dream too big and don't make it, you might be discouraged when it comes to accomplishing other goals. If you set attainable goals and meet them, you'll be more inspired to set more goals you can reach.

11. Use your imagination.

Don't restrict yourself to straightforward business practices – use your imagination! Take a creative approach to your projects and presentations, and brainstorm any task you're given to see how you can blow your bosses out of the water.

12. Don't beat yourself up over mistakes.

If you make a mistake, whether it's a verbal slip-up in a meeting or a typo in an email, let it go. You can't beat yourself up over something like that, because everyone makes mistakes. Don't forget what you've done wrong, but learn from it and move on. Take comfort in the fact that people won't remember it for long, and use it to push yourself to do better next time, so instead of remembering your blunder, they'll remember your success!

13. Reward yourself for your accomplishments.

Every time you finish a task, pat yourself on the back. When you finish a major project, treat yourself to dinner out or a new movie. It's just as important to reward yourself for your accomplishments as it is to not beat yourself up over mistakes. Marking something off your To Do list feels good enough as it is, but if you reward yourself, even with something small, you'll be proud of yourself and want to accomplish more.

14. Surround yourself with positive people.

Stay away from coworkers who bring their negative energy into your life and your workspace. It might be difficult to avoid people if you work in close quarters with them, but you can at least make all of your interactions with them positive by keeping upbeat. Your positive attitude might help them change their tune!

15. Smile more.

Smile when you greet your coworkers and clients. Smile when you walk down the hall. Smile even when you don't want to smile, and see how much it improves your days! Smiling even if you don't feel happy will make you feel better, and seeing a smile on your face will make others feel better, too!

You can do anything you put your mind to it. You have many people behind you, including me. You are strong, and you are stronger than you will ever know! So keep going strong!

Live in this moment, enjoy every second of it, those moments together will make the perfect happy life. There is a certain magic in those little moments, standing by the sea, staring down from the top of a mountain. Let them sway and guide you.

The things you notice the least tend to impact you the most. Look for the sights and sounds just outside your periphery.

www.ingramcontent.com/pod-product-compliance
Lightning Source LLC
Chambersburg PA
CBHW030533220526
45463CB00007B/2816